Beginners Guide to
Investing

Free membership into the Mastermind Self Development Group!

For a limited time, you can join the Mastermind Self Development Group for free! You will receive videos and articles from top authorities in self development as well as a special group only offers on new books and training programs. There will also be a monthly member only draw that gives you a chance to win any book from your Kindle wish list!

If you sign up through this link http://www.mastermindselfdevelopment.com/specialreport you will also get a special free report on the Wheel of Life. This report will give you a visual look at your current life and then take you through a series of exercises that will help you plan what your perfect life looks like. The workbook does not end there; we then take you through a process to help you plan how to achieve that perfect life. The process is very powerful and has the potential to change your life forever. Join the group now and start to change your life! http://www.mastermindselfdevelopment.com/specialreport

Introduction

Introduction

Money is an extremely important part of our lives. We need money to buy things, pay for services and also reserve some for the future. However, the salary we earn ends up being too less, owing to growing inflation and increasing needs.

So what can we do to increase our monthly income and have enough money for the future? Well, investing your money is a good choice it will help your money's worth increase over time.

There are several investment options to choose from but none of them prove to be as enticing and lucrative as stock market investments.

Stock market investments refer to investing your money in buying financial securities that are traded in the share exchange market. These investments are easy to make and you can easily increase your monthly income.

But in order to invest, you must have enough knowledge about these markets and know exactly how to invest in them. There are many small, and big, details to consider before you start investing your money in the stock market.

In this book, we will look at the stock market in detail and understand everything that there is to, about stocks, bonds, etfs and precious metals. We will also look at some tips for you to manage your money and trade wisely.

I hope this book helps you in making the right financial choices for yourself.

I want to thank you for choosing this book and hope you enjoy it.

Chapter 1: Stock Market Basics

The stock market is a big market place, where financial securities are traded on a daily basis. People, worldwide, buy and sell these securities every day, in order to earn an income from them. If you have watched the movie, "The wolf of wall street", you will have a fair idea of how the stock market operates.

In this chapter, we will look at some of the basic concepts that relate to the stock market.

What is it?

The stock market is a physical market where companies list their stocks. These companies can be big or small and will float their shares in the market. These shares are bought and sold on a daily basis. Apart from company shares, other financial securities such as bonds, etfs, commodities and precious metals are also traded in the share market. There is a separate market for each and you can trade in all of them or some of them depending on your needs.

There are two types of markets namely the physical market and the virtual market. The physical market is where brokers trade in stocks on the floor of the market. The most famous physical market in the world is the New York Stock Exchange or NYSE. Here, many multi national companies from all over the world list their stocks for people to buy and sell. If you wish to trade here then you have to be a member of the stock exchange.

The other type of stock market is known as the virtual market. These virtual markets are online markets and you can trade in them by creating an account. There are no brokers here and you can buy and sell by interacting with other members of the stock market. The most famous online stock market is NASDAQ.

You can choose to trade in any of these markets or both.

Basic components

There are many components in the stock market but only a few of them are basic namely the stock markets, the brokerage firms, the brokers and the demat account. Let us look at each one in detail.

Stock market

As you know, the stock market is a place where you buy and sell financial instruments. It is a market place where buyers and sellers meet to satisfy their investment needs. It can be a physical or a virtual market. You can trade in any one of them or both. There are many stock markets all over the world and that are all inter linked owing to sharing common stocks.

Brokerage firms

As was mentioned earlier, you need to be a member of the stock market if you wish to buy and sell shares. But it is not easy to become a member and you have to pay a lot of money to do so. So instead, you can sign up with a brokerage firm and trade in the market. There are many firms to choose from and you must look for the best one that is well reputed.

Brokers

Brokers are employed with brokerage firms and will help you buy and sell shares. They will charge a commission for their services. There are two types of brokers, one being full time brokers and the other being part time brokers. Full time brokers will dedicatedly work for you and invest your money. Part time brokers will only buy and sell your stocks and will not assist you in the decision making process. You must pick a broker based on your requirements.

Demat account

The demat account is what you will need to trade with in the stock market. This account is not like you regular bank account. There was a time when it took people several days to buy and sell stocks. But now, it takes only a few seconds to do so. This is only possible if you have a demat account.

Basic terminologies

Here are some basic terms that you must get acquainted with to start trading in the stock market.

Stocks: Stocks are shares of companies that are sold in the stock market. These shares will help a person own a part of the company. Stocks are the most preferred stock market investment choices.

Bonds: Bonds are financial instruments that are either listed by companies or the government. Bonds are issued to the customer at a value that is much lower than its face value.

Etfs: ETFs stand for exchange transfer funds. ETFs are like mutual funds but traded in the stock market. They are like regular stocks but with the benefits of a mutual fund.

Precious metals: Precious metals are also traded in the stock market these include gold, silver, platinum etc. These are traded on a daily basis just like stocks.

Commodities: commodities are every goods and items that are traded in the stock market. There are many categories of commodities like livestock and energy that are all traded in the stock market.

Foreign exchange: foreign exchange refers to foreign currency that is traded in the stock market. These are foreign currencies that are traded on a daily basis.

Basic techniques of trade

Intra day trading

Intraday trading refers to trading in the stock market on a daily basis. You can buy and sell stocks daily. This is an advanced form of trading and you must take it up only after studying the stock market for some time. The risk and reward are both quite high in this form of trading and you can undertake it to earn a daily income.

Short term trading

Short term trading, as the name suggests, refers to trading for a period less than 6 months. So you buy and hold a financial instrument for less than 6 months and then dispose it off. Short term trading is a lot like intra day trading as the time period varies between a week and 6 months.

Long term trading

Long term trading refers to holding a stock for a long time. This time will vary from instrument to instrument. This is said to be a safe option and will give you consistent returns provided you invest in the best stocks and other instruments.

Chapter 2: FAQs On The Topic

It is obvious that you will have a few doubts, when you take up a new topic. In this chapter, we will look at the various FAQs on the subject and understand the topic of stock markets better.

What is trading in the stock market?

Stock market trading refers to buying and selling stocks. These stocks are valued at a certain price and the basic intent is to capitalize on its revised price. So you must buy a stock at a low price and then sell it at a higher value. There are many categories of stocks to choose from including IT, pharma, construction etc. You must sign up with a brokerage firm and then start trading in shares. Apart from these shares, there are many other financial instruments that are traded in the market. We will look at each one in detail in the chapters to come.

Who is it for?

Stock market investments are for everybody, interested in increasing their capital's worth. The market does not discriminate and anybody can partake in the buying and selling. As long as you have the capital for it and are willing to take a risk, you can take part in the stock market. Right from working professionals to students to housewives, the stock market welcomes everybody with open arms. But before you decide to invest in it, you must understand everything that there is to and only then start trading in stocks and other financial securities. That you can do by going through this book and reading on the stock market essentials.

Is it a safe choice?

No investment is a safe choice and everything comes with a certain amount of risk attached with it. If you think it is a safe bet for you to invest in the stock market then you are wrong. There are many things that can go wrong and you must be prepared for them. If you tread cautiously then you will not experience any problems. But that does not mean they are not present. It is of utmost importance that you understand carefully all the different concepts and only then can you decide to jump into the stock market. So basically, there are no guarantees in the market but you can minimize the risk by making smart choices for yourself.

Can I become rich overnight?

This is a big misconception that many people have when it comes to stock market investments. They assume that they can capitalize on a few good stocks and double or triple their money. But as I said, it's a misconception and the stock market will not make anyone rich over night. Patience is extremely important and you will have to wait it out before realizing any substantial profits. If you are in a hurry to see results then you will end up settling for a loss. So don't have unreasonable expectations from the stock market.

Is it a full time job?

Not necessarily. If you employ a broker then he or she will buy and sell your stocks so that you can only pick the stocks and the time to buy and sell. But if you wish to do intraday trading then you might have to take it up full time as the prices of stocks change every second and you have to make quick decisions. If you think your stock market trade is going very well then you can consider taking it up full time and making it your day job.

Can I buy and sell by myself?

Yes. Although you need to sign up with a brokerage firm, you can buy and sell stocks by yourself. You need not always rely on your broker to buy and sell your stocks. You might end up wasting time in doing so. You will be given access to your demat account and you can start trading by yourself. It might take you some time to understand how it works but once you get down to doing it, it will start getting relatively easier for you.

Will I be charged for it?

Yes. You will be charged a minimum commission by the brokering firm, as you will be using their services. So even if you refuse to take the help of the broker, you will still have to pay a fee for it. But that is only fair given you are using the firm's membership in the stock market to buy and sell your stocks. If they weren't present then you wouldn't have the chance to buy and sell stocks. The choice is fully yours. You can choose to employ the services of the broker or buy and sell the stocks by yourself.

How long will results take?

Results will not take long to show provided you do all the right things. Patience is vital and you will have to study the markets for some time before investing in the stock market. If you try to hurry things up then you will have to settle for a compromise. Understand that it is your hard earned money being invested in the market and you must do all the right things for it. Don't have unreasonable expectations from it as the higher the expectation, the higher the disappointment. So don't expect to get rich overnight and have a little patience.

What's the best choice to pick?

That depends on you. Individual choices vary and what works for one will not work for another. So don't choose an option just because someone else is choosing it. If you think the option will work well for you then pick it. Most people prefer to diversify their portfolio and have each of the elements in their choice of investments. You can do the same but don't rush into all of it. Take it slow and move to the next financial security only after you have fully exploited one option.

Can I quit anytime?

Yes. Starting and quitting is up to you. But don't quit when you have a lot of debt in the stock market. Quit only because you are satisfied with your investments. If you think you can create a lot of debts and run away from it then you will only get yourself into a lot of trouble. So don't be in a hurry to join and quit the stock market. Think out your decisions carefully and ensure that you know exactly what you are getting into.

These form the various questions that beginners ask about the stock market and I hope you had yours answered successfully.

Chapter 3: Stocks Basics

In the previous chapter, we looked at some questions and answers that will help you understand the topic of stock market better. In this chapter, we will read on the basics of stocks, their types and their various advantages and disadvantages to consider before choosing them.

What are they?

A stock is basically a share of the company. A share refers to a part of the company including its finances and every other asset that it owns. When the company decides to go public with its shares, it announces an IPO or initial public offering. Anybody interested in buying the shares will then approach the company and pay the share value to own the shares. This is known as primary selling. These shares are then sold in the share market. The share market is a huge place where buyers and sellers converge to conduct daily trade. These shares are then bought and sold and the seller capitalizes on the current price of the share, which will be much higher than what he had bought it at. The buyer will have the chance to capitalize on the share once its value rises.

Companies decide to go public with their shares due to many reasons. But the main reason is to raise capital for their business. So they will value their company and split the shares. They will then value individual shares depending on their market capture and asset to liability ratio. A small company might capture a big market share and a big company might capture a small share. It depends on the individual company's board members' decision.

So say A has 100 shares of Microsoft priced at $20 each. He will sell it to B who has to pay $2000 for it. Now B is holding on to it in a bid to sell it for $25 or $30 and make a profit on it.

The stock market is huge and there are many companies that list their shares. As an investor, you must choose the best one for yourself and invest wisely.

Types of stocks

Stocks are of two main types namely Common stock and Preferred stock. These types are different from each other and each one has a unique characteristic. You can choose either one after evaluating their meaning and characteristics.

Common stock

Also known as equity stocks, common stocks are what are mostly traded in the stock market. These are second hand stocks that the previous owners have pumped into the stock market. Common stock holders are generally placed at the bottom of the ownership staircase. They will be considered last if the time to payout comes by. So in case the company is winding up, these will be compensated last after the other stockholders have been paid in full. But these stocks are cheap and easily available and are ideal for short term trading. The only gain from these will be a dividend pay out or an earning from the difference in their share prices. Owners of this stock have the right to elect the board of members.

Preferred stocks

Preferred stocks are first hand stocks. These are considered first in case there is liquidation in the company. So it is a safe bet to buy such stocks. However, the holders have no right in electing the board of members in the company. But these stocks will help the holders avail a fixed rate of dividend regardless of the company undergoing profits or losses. So these stocks are much preferred.

These are the two types of shares available in the market and you can choose the best one depending on your analysis and needs.

Advantages of stocks

It is a good idea to invest in stocks, as there are many advantages to it. The first advantage is that you will avail a certain monthly income in the form of dividends that are paid out by the company. Although a single company will only pay once every quarter, you can hold stocks of as many companies as you like and have a consistent income. Another advantage is the choices that it gives you. You can either hold it for just a single day or hold it for years together. You don't have to dispose off what you buy immediately and can hold on to it if you think it will grow in value over time. Their liquidity is what makes them highly suited for both small and large investments. If you end up buying the stocks of a company that is on the verge of booming, then you will have the chance to be part owner of an extremely profitable company. Also, when you have your money invested in the stock market, you will not be able to withdraw from it easily. This is great for all those that have the habit of withdrawing money often and spending it unnecessarily.

Disadvantages of stocks

Just like the advantages, there are also certain disadvantages of investing in the stock market. The first one being volatility. As you know, the stock market is a very volatile place where the prices keep fluctuating every second. A good stock today might end up at the bottom of the pile tomorrow and your investment might get jeopardized. These stocks fluctuate owing to the demand and supply and it will be very difficult for you to predict these. In fact, what most stock investors find frustrating is how the prices can vary without any apparent reason and cause you losses. Another disadvantage is that it is not easy to get your hands on preferred stocks. So as common stock holders, you might not know everything that there is to about the company.

These form the various advantages and disadvantages of stocks and you can choose to invest in them if you think you have enough risk capital at your disposal.

Chapter 4: Bonds Basics

In the previous chapter, we read in detail about stocks, their types, advantages and disadvantages, in this chapter, we will do the same with Bonds.

What are they?

Bonds and stocks are often mentioned in the same breath but they differ drastically in terms of their structure and payouts. So comparing the two is wrong and will leave the investor confused.

Bonds are issues by companies to the public when they wish to raise money for their business. As you know, multi national companies will require a lot of capital for their day-to-day use and also to fund any new project. They will not always have this money readily available with them and will have to turn to other sources. Although there are many finance providing institutions such as banks and moneylenders, they will not be ready to finance a large amount of money.

So the best choice for these companies is to raise the money from the public. They will issue bonds to them for a fixed period of time after which they will pay out the entire sum borrowed along with a rate of interest. They might also agree to pay a monthly interest instead of paying it in lump sum. The value of the bond will be much lesser than its actual face value. So if the person wishes to dispose off the bond before its maturity then he will get paid a higher sum for it.

Bonds are said to be slightly more secure options as compared to stocks as there is no volatility. The pay out period is also pre determined so the person does not have to worry about holding on to the bonds for a long time.

Types of bonds

There are 5 main types of bonds and they are as follows:

Corporate bonds

As the name suggests, corporate bonds are issued by companies to the public. They will have to raise money for their company's projects and so, will issue bonds for the public. The public will then buy these by paying a certain amount of money. The company will promise to pay back the amount in say 2 years' time and in the meant time, pay a 10% interest on it. The main advantage of this type of investment is that, you will win over the company's loyalty. So they might end up issuing free shares to you at a low rate, which will allow you to become part owner of the company.

Government bonds

Government bonds are issued by the federal government. Just like the corporates, the government will also require money to fund its projects. And so, they will issue bonds to the public in a bid to raise money for themselves. You can buy these bonds and hold on to them until they reach their maturity period or dispose them off before that if you are in need of money. Even if you dispose them off, you will still get paid more than what you ha paid for them and you will transfer all your rights to the buyer of the bond.

Agency bonds

Agency bonds refer to those that are issued by affiliates of the government. So they are issued by those companies that are backed by the government but are not run by them. They will also issue bonds to raise money for their business. The same rules apply here as well where you can sell the bond to someone and get paid extra or hold on to it and earn a certain interest every month. Although these are backed by the government, they don't come with the same guarantees that government bonds come with. So ensure that you thoroughly read the terms and conditions first before investing in them!

Municipal bonds

Just like the federal government, the various local and state governments will also issue bonds to the public to raise money for its projects. These are also safe options to pick and you can earn a substantial rate of interest for your investment, which will be much higher than what your bank would pay you. Municipal bonds are some of the preferred types of bonds in the share market.

Zero coupon bonds

Zero coupon bonds are those that are valued much lesser than their actual value and the issued to you. After a while, they are bought back at their actual value. So if you bought a bond at $500, whose actual price is $800, you will get paid in full for it after 2 years. So you can realize a profit of $300 from it at a later date. These are safe options for you to pick for yourself.

Advantages of bonds

The main advantage of bonds is that, there are many guarantees attached to them. The first guarantee is that you will get back your money for sure, provided you invest in government bonds. The next guarantee is that you will receive a fixed rate of interest on your investment, which is extremely important for an investor. Bonds can be issued within a few minutes and you don't have to wait for too long for the investment to go through. These guarantees are not available with your share investments.

Disadvantages of bonds

The main disadvantage of bonds is the rate of return on your investment will not be as high as what the stock market will provide you. You will have to settle for a low rate and wait for years together before getting back your principle sum. The guarantees are always only associated with government bonds and you will not have any for your corporate and agency bonds. Even if they do pay you more than what the government bonds would, you will have to risk it all if you invest in corporate bonds.

These form the various advantages and disadvantages of investing in bonds and you can pick them depending on your needs and expectations from your investments.

You are halfway done!

Congratulations on making it to the halfway point of the journey. Many try and give up long before even getting to this point, so you are to be congratulated on this. You have shown that you are serious about getting better every day. I am also serious about improving my life, and helping others get better along the way. To do this I need your feedback. Click on the link below and take a moment to let me know how this book has helped you. If you feel there is something missing or something you would like to see differently, I would love to know about it. I want to ensure that as you and I improve, this book continues to improve as well. Thank you for taking the time to ensure that we are all getting the most from each other.

Chapter 5: ETFs, Options And Commodities Basics

By now, we have looked at stocks and bonds in detail. In this chapter, we will look at ETFs and options and understand the different concepts associated with them.

What are they?

Etfs stand for exchange transfer funds. These funds are a lot like mutual funds but are traded in the stock market. So a company will invest a part of their investment in different financial securities and then split up the investments into individual units. These are then bought and sold in the share market like regular stocks. But the difference is that you can buy and sell them on the same day as opposed to remaining invested in them for 3 to 5 years.

Types of ETFs

There are 6 main types of etfs that you can choose from and they are as follows.

Equity etfs

These etfs are those that will follow the pattern of the index. So, it will be a small sample of the index, like Amex, and you will possess a slice of the market when you buy yourself this etf.

Real estate etfs

As the name suggests, real estate etf is one where you will hold the shares of a company that invests in real estate projects. Since they are majorly being funded by the public, they will compulsorily have to declare 90% of their profits to the public. These are better known as Real estate Investment trusts and they are safe options for you to choose for your investments.

Currency etfs

These are foreign currency stocks. When you invest in these, you will be safeguarding your money against any inflation or deflation that might affect dollar value. You will also have the chance to make a foreign investment, which will diversify your portfolio. So these etfs are great for you.

Commodity etfs

Commodity etfs refer to those that are predominantly invested in the commodities market. So when you buy these, you will own a share in the commodities market but will not have to speculate and get dispose it off it, when it reaches your target price.

Fixed income etfs

These are better known as bond etfs. Here, you will receive a certain fixed rate of interest owing to owning etfs that correspond to bonds in the stock market.

Specialty etfs

These are special etfs that are formulated to help the investor avail a double or triple return on investment. These are also good choices for both beginners and old hands.

Advantages of ETFs

The main advantage of investing in etfs is that, they will provide you with the benefits of investing in mutual funds but give you the chance to trade them on a daily basis. So you can capture several different elements of the stock market at once and buy and sell them at the same time. The other advantage is risk diversification. By investing in etfs, you are diversifying your risk and are not investing in just one form of investment.

Disadvantages of ETFs

The disadvantage of etfs is that, you will not have the chance to make a lot of money on it and the rate of return on your investment will be very low. So, you might end up getting less than 5% return on your over all investment. Another disadvantage of etfs is that, they will move extremely slowly. They will move like snails and you will not be able to capitalize on their speed.

Options

Options, on the other hand, are schemes where you can reserve a financial security and not pay for them immediately. So say for example you wish to purchase a stock worth $50 and want 100 of them. Instead of paying $5000 for it, you tell the seller you will reserve the stock by paying $1000 for it. The seller will agree provided you pay in full within the agreed time period. Now say in a week's time, you realize that the stock belongs to a very good company and its value has risen to $60 per share. You can immediately pay the remaining money and buy the stock at the agreed price. The seller is forced to give it away at the lower price owing to his commitment.

On the other hand, suppose the price of the stock drops to $40 owing to internal issues in the company. You have agreed to pay $50 per share and if you are to sell it now, you will only get $40 for it. So here, you have the option to not pay in full at all and wipe your hands off of it. But you will have to lose the $1000 that you had paid as advance for it. This is still a good option, given how you will be saving $4000 on it.

Types of options

Options are of two main types viz. American options and European options

American options

American options are those that are extensively practiced in the market. This is a flexible option and is ideal for new and old investors. American options will give you the chance to sell your option at any time before the arrival of the maturity date. So you can encash on the stock's high price and sell it sometime before its maturity. So say for example you bought options of company A where you paid $500 as advance and wish to sell the stock for a $500 profit. The maturity date for the stock is 1 March 2016. If the opportunity presents itself for you to sell it on 1 October 2015 and realize a profit on it then you can take that option for yourself.

European options

European options are the next type of options that you can choose for yourself. These are not as flexible as American options, and are extremely rigid. They will only allow you to dispose them off after they have reached the maturity period. If in between you have the chance to capitalize on its value then you won't have the chance to do so. European options are not popular but they are available for you to choose.

Note: These are mere names for the options and have no geographic relevance.

Advantages of options

Options are great as the investment is quite safe. Even if you do end up losing the reservation money, you are still getting away with not paying the agreed amount. The rewards that options pay are high and possibly highest as compared to other forms of investments. Options are also easy to understand and operate and are ideal for beginners to understand how the stock market works.

Disadvantages of options

The major disadvantage of options is that it will be difficult to speculate. You will think the price will rise but it will end up falling and you will decide to pass on the date and not honor the deal and the price will rise up. So, it is difficult to understand when and how the prices of the security will rise and fall. Also, the reservation money will still be your hard earned money and having to lose it unnecessarily will hurt you financially.

Commodities

Commodities refer to everyday commodities that are bought and sold in the stock market. These are valued at a certain price and then you can sell them at a higher price. This is a form of speculative trade just like options trading. You can pick a certain commodity and then buy and sell it before its expiry date. Commodities trading are an advanced form of trading and you must take it up after careful evaluation.

Types of commodities

Energy: These are energies such as oil and gas. You will have to buy them at a certain price and then speculate on a future price. As soon as that price is reached, you can sell them. The difference will be your profit. These resources are rare and so, they will be priced highly.

Livestock*: Livestock such as pig and chicken and meats such as pork are also traded in the market. You have to speculate on their price as well and then buy them. These are slightly less volatile and things such as weather conditions and market demand will affect them.

Metals*: Metals such as iron, zinc and nickel are also traded. These are heavily used in industries and so; their market demand will be quite high. You must buy them at a certain price and then wait for their price to go up before selling them.

Agriculture*: This is the most widely traded commodity in the market. Agricultural produce such as sugar, rice and vegetables are traded in the market. You will have to buy them in quintals to trade with them.

Advantages of commodities

The main advantage of investing in commodities is that, it is a safe option to invest in. Even during times of crisis, your commodities will remain safe and so will your investments. The returns that you earn from your commodities investments is also quite high, which is an added advantage. You can further diversify your business by investing in commodities. You must remain patient and understand the trade carefully to realize a profit on your investment.

Disadvantages of commodities

The main disadvantage of this form of investment is that, you will be willing to take a greater risk on your investment and end up creating losses for yourself. Another disadvantage is that the prices keep fluctuating too fast. So buy the time you decide to capitalize on a price, it would have shifted and you will end up losing money.

These for the various advantages and disadvantages of etfs, options and commodities and you must decide on one depending on your needs and capacity.

Chapter 6: Precious Metals And Foreign Exchange Basics

Stocks, bonds, etfs and options are all virtual securities. Apart from these, there are two other types that will give you a physical possession of your investments.

In this chapter, we will look at these two chapters in detail.

What are they?

Precious metals are gold, silver and platinum, which are traded in the stock market just like regular stocks. They are also valued at a certain price and traded in the bullion market. When you buy and sell these, you are looking to capitalize on its difference in value.

These metals are extensively used in the jewelry industry and also several other industries. This makes it extremely valuable and so, its prices keep going up and down all day long. So it is important to remain alert and observe the trends consistently and then invest in them.

Precious metals

Here are three of the most traded precious metals in the market

Gold: Gold as you know is extremely valuable. The yellow metal is used to make jewelry and also finds its use in the dental industry. You can either buy it in the form of coins or bars or also buy jewelry if you prefer that. But jewelry is not as valuable considering its weight will be less and the maker will charge you for its making. However, it cannot be ruled out as a good investment.

Silver: Silver is also a valuable precious metal. It finds its use in several industries. So the price will keep fluctuating all through the day. But the price per kg for silver is much lower than it is for gold and you can buy more of it.

Platinum: Platinum is the costliest of all precious metals. It is used in jewelry and many industries. Even with a large investment, you will only get a little platinum. So you have to buy it at the lowest price possible.

There is no time limit and you can hold these precious metals for as long as you like.

Advantages of precious metals

The main advantage of buying precious metals is that, you will get physical custody of your investment. Precious metals are extremely valuable and an investment here will be a safe option. You can sell your precious metals at any time and make money on it.

Another advantage is that the prices will be global and you can exchange your precious metals for cash in any part of the world.

Disadvantages of precious metals

One disadvantage of buying precious metals is that, you will have to start with a big investment. Even so, you can only buy a little and make do with it. Remember that the higher the investment, the higher the return.

Foreign currencies

Foreign currencies are exchanged just as precious metals. Each of these currencies has a certain value, which will be higher or lower when compared to other currencies. When you buy the currencies of one country, you can exchange it for another countries currency and come into a profit.

Advantages of foreign currencies

The main advantage of buying and selling foreign currencies is that, the market is extremely big and you can capitalize on its diversity. You can buy and sell many currencies on the same day.

Disadvantages of foreign currencies

The disadvantage of dealing in foreign currencies is that, you have to adjust to the other countries times if you want to trade consistently.

Chapter 7: Money Management Tips

As you know, it is not enough for you to understand the basics of investing and must know to manage it properly. You cannot keep investing unless you have enough money saved up for yourself.

So to educate you on matters of money management, we will look at some things that you must do today!

Budgeting

Preparing a budget is extremely important. A budget is meant to help you keep track of your incomes and expenses. When you track these, you know whether you are spending properly or are over spending your money.

The basics of a budget involve recording your incomes on one side and your expenses on the other. Draw out a table and mention all the incomes on one side and the expenses on the other. Now tally both and see which one is higher. If the incomes are higher then you are left with a surplus and if the expense total is higher, then you have a deficit.

It is important for you to always have a surplus as that means you are spending less than what you are making. This surplus can be saved. But if you have a deficit, then you will have to reduce it and try and match your expenses and incomes. Then you further cut down on unnecessary expenditures and create a surplus.

Saving

Saving money is the second step that you must take towards managing your money efficiently. You cannot invest if you don't have savings. So before getting into the stock market, make sure you have enough money saved up with you. These savings can be in the form of bank deposits or bonds. Both of them will return your money back to you after attaching a certain interest. But you must choose places that offer you good rate of interest. Decide on a number, like $10,000 and ensure that your savings reach that mark. Only then should you decide to start investing your money in the market.

I know it is easier said than done, as not everybody will have the motivation to save money. So the best thing to do is reward yourself every time you put money into the savings account. Mind you, this should be surplus money that will only supplement whatever money you have decided to directly transfer from your checking account to your savings account on a monthly basis. If you have a spouse or a partner then ask them to do the same.

Safe investments

When it comes to savings, ensure that you trust only reliable sources. Many people decide to trust frauds and end up losing their hard earned money. There will be several fraudsters and scammers out there who will prey on innocent victims and dupe them. They will not appear to be scammers and will look extremely innocent. You have to be wary of such people and stay as away from their fraudulent schemes. Even if it is a colleague or someone you know, don't enter any scheme without conducting due research.

Trading

When it comes to trading in the stock market, you have to be very careful. You must not make silly mistakes, which will cause you to lose money instead of gaining. Losing money is never an option and you must put in all efforts to increase your money's worth. Don't be over enthusiastic and plan everything out in advance. Come up with a plan of action to follow. Stick to your plan and don't deviate from it. You can take the help of a friend to plan out your finances and then invest it in all the best places.

Retirement planning

Remember that you must plan for your retirement. You must have enough money saved up to lead a comfortable life. You must not depend on others for your financial needs. Start with a plan and follow through with it. You must also contribute towards your 401(k). Have your own house and your own car as well. These are basic things but you must pay attention to them if you wish to retire in peace.

These form just some of the money management tips for you to follow but are not limited to just these.

Chapter 8: Trading Tips

In the previous chapter, we looked at some money management tips for you. It is important that you manage your money in the best possible way and understand the value of increasing its potential over time.

Learn daily

The stock market is a place where every day new stories are made. If you think you have seen it all, then you are absolutely wrong! Treat every day as a new day and every incident as a learning curve to take away a lesson from it. What you learn today will benefit you tomorrow and so on and so forth. Don't assume things for yourself and make a note of all the incidents that you face. Even if it is a bad situation, learn to take a lesson from it. It might be a temporary phase but you must consider it a threat at all times.

Invest risk capital

When it comes to stock market investments, remember that you are investing real money that you will have to risk. So, invest whatever you are willing to lose. Better known as risk capital, you have to calculate your risk and know exactly how much you might end up losing in the market. It's obvious that you will not always lose the money but it is best to be prepared for the worst. Another piece of advice is to always invest your own money and not somebody else's money. Even if someone willfully gives you the money to spend, you will still be responsible for it and it will be impossible for you to predict the future and your stocks might end up crashing which is a very big risk.

Own mind

Remember to always have your own mind when it comes to investing in the stock market. If you rely too much on others for their advice and opinions, then you will end up making mistakes. You will have two opinions to work with and remain confused all the time. So don't trust others too much and simply consider their opinion once. When you hear about a good stock, do your own research for it instead of blindly trusting the news. Many times, the news will turn out to be a hoax. So be careful and not blindly trust everything you hear from others, everybody if they are experts.

Be prepared

When it comes to the stock market, you have to mentally prepare for it. Remain ready to take a loss on some of the stocks, as you cannot always remain in profit. The best thing to do is maintain a 5% loss risk in all stocks and not any more. You will have to make use of a technique known as stop loss, where you decide how much loss you can take on a stock. Don't worry if you take loss on a few stocks in a row. It's just an indication that you should take it slow and start trading wisely. You will know to invest wisely and not make the same mistakes over and over again.

Diversify

Diversification is an extremely important part of your stock market investments. When you diversify, you spread out your risk and profit. If you invest everything in the same place, you have to settle for anything that it offers you regardless of good or bad. But if you spread your risk, then you will have to bear only a little and your other investments can save you. Many beginners make the mistake of investing in just one type of security and don't consider diversifying. But you don't make that mistake and try to maintain as diverse a portfolio as possible.

Timing

Timing the market is essential. There are clear times when it will be best to buy a security and hold it and times when it will be good to sell them. You have to understand the difference in the timings and invest wisely. Don't be in a hurry to make the decisions. Nobody is asking you to buy and sell within a few seconds. Take your time to analyze and assess a situation before making a decision. It will be a little difficult in the beginning but nothing that you cannot learn to do.

Understand brokerage

Remember that it is a compulsion for you to sign up with a brokering firm to trade in the stock market. If you don't, then you cannot trade at all. So find the best firm for yourself and ensure that you pay only a little towards them as the commission. Many people end up paying a lot of money as commission, which eats away into their profits. So check the rate of commission first and then sign up with them. You will avoid a lot of unnecessary arguments and problems by doing so.

No love

Remember to never get too attached with a financial security. People end up falling in love with a company and refuse to let go of their stocks. Similarly, they will get attached to gold and not wish to sell it even if a lucrative offer comes by. So leave love and emotions out of it and focus only on your profits and losses. You have to remain mentally and emotionally strong and remain as away from establishing a bonding as possible with all your stocks.

Penny stocks

Penny stocks refer to those stocks that are valued at less than $5. These stocks are said to be good investments but only if you know to trade in them. Don't buy them if you don't know how to trade intraday. They will rise and fall within a single day and you have to be quick in making your decisions. Penny stocks can make you rich and poor in a matter of seconds and so, you have to invest in them only if you have the confidence to handle their volatility.

Expectations

It is obvious that you will have certain expectations from your stock market investments. Some will have high expectations and some will have low. But it is best to find a middle path and have limited expectations out of it. These should not be too high or too low and must lie somewhere in between.

These form the different trading tips that you must understand and incorporate to make the most of your investments.

Key Takeaways

When you wish to invest in the stock market, you have to start with the very basics. You cannot simply jump into it without knowing anything about it. Start by understanding how the stock market operates and acquaint yourself with all the different terms that are used in the trade. These details will help make your stock market journey easier.

Understanding the different risks that the stock market throws at you is important to know. Remember that no investment guarantees anything and you have to be prepared for the worst. But don't get scared, it is only a precautionary measure and it is best to calculate your risk when you wish to invest money in the stock market.

Stocks are the first type of investments to consider. Stocks are shares of the company and when someone buys them, they own a part of the company. These shares are listed in the stock market and are bought and sold on a daily basis. You can indulge in intraday trading or long-term investments.

Bonds are the next choice that you can pick. Bonds are issued by governments or corporates and you can buy them at a lower face value and sell them at a higher price. The best way to pick bonds is by going by recommendations. You can invest in them for a year or more and it is best suited for those looking for consistent returns.

Etfs are like mutual funds but traded on the stock market. You can buy and sell them on a daily basis and capitalize on its price difference. Etfs are generally slow moving so you will have to wait for it to rise in value over a period of time. But don't give up on them too early as once they begin to pick up speed, you can capitalize on it.

Options are investments that will allow you to stick with your deal or walk away from it. So you can choose to either stay put with your commitment or walk away from it. But there is a catch. You will have to pay a certain sum as a reservation amount and will have to let go of it if you wish to walk away from the deal. So you need to be careful while picking options.

Commodities are traded on the market every day. There are metals, livestock, agricultural products and energy resources, which are listed in the market. You can buy them at a certain price and then sell them when they increase in value. Commodities help you diversify your portfolio.

Precious metals are like commodities except that you can get physical possession after buying them. Here too, you must capitalize on their price variations. You can hold on to your precious metals for as long as you like.

Foreign currencies are also traded on a daily basis. One country's currency will always be lesser or higher in value as compared to another country's currency. You must capitalize on this difference to earn from it.

Managing money is extremely important. It is not enough if you investment money. You have to start with savings. Prepare a monthly budget and devise a savings plan. Once you have enough savings, you can start investing.

When you enter the stock market, take it slow and don't be in a hurry to make money. If you go too fast then you will end up making unnecessary mistakes. Make use of precautionary measures to safeguard your investments.

Conclusion

I thank you once again for choosing this book and hope you had a good time reading it.

The main aim of this book was to educate you on the basics of the stock market. As you can see, there are many things to learn, and understand, before you start investing in the stock market. But once you understand these thoroughly, you will be able to invest and realize a profit on your capital investments.

The next step is for you to incorporate these ideals and start investing your money in the stock market and hope you find success.

All the best!

Free membership into the Mastermind Self Development Group!

For a limited time, you can join the Mastermind Self Development Group for free! You will receive videos and articles from top authorities in self development as well as a special group only offers on new books and training programs. There will also be a monthly member only draw that gives you a chance to win any book from your Kindle wish list!

If you sign up through this link http://www.mastermindselfdevelopment.com/specialreport you will also get a special free report on the Wheel of Life. This report will give you a visual look at your current life and then take you through a series of exercises that will help you plan what your perfect life looks like. The workbook does not end there; we then take you through a process to help you plan how to achieve that perfect life. The process is very powerful and has the potential to change your life forever. Join the group now and start to change your life! http://www.mastermindselfdevelopment.com/specialreport